D0461593

Science Experiments

Wild & Wacky Science Experiments

WATERBIRD BOOKS

Columbus, Ohio

President: Vincent F. Douglas

Publisher: Tracey E. Dils

Project Editors: Joanna Callihan and Nathan Hemmelgarn

Contributors: Q.L. Pearce, Barbara Saffer, Ph.D., Tony Gleeson, Leo Abbett, Tim Harkins, and Neal Yamamoto

Art Directors: Robert Sanford and Christopher Fowler

Interior Design and Production: Jennifer Bowers

Cover Design: Jennifer Bowers

Align to Achieve
The Academic Standards e-Library

This product has been aligned to state and national organization standards using the Align to Achieve Standards Database. Align to Achieve, Inc., is an independent, not-for-profit organization that facilitates the evaluation and improvement of academic standards and student achievement. To find how this product aligns to your standards, go to www.MHstandards.com.

Mc Graw Hill Children's Publishing

© 2004 McGraw-Hill Children's Publishing.

This edition published in the United States of America in 2003 by Waterbird Books,
an imprint of McGraw-Hill Children's Publishing,
a Division of The McGraw-Hill Companies
8787 Orion Place
Columbus, Ohio 43240-4027

www.MHkids.com

Library of Congress Cataloging-in-Publication Data is on file with the publisher.

Printed in the United States of America.

1-57768-625-X

1 2 3 4 5 6 7 8 9 10 PHXBK 09 08 07 06 05 04 03

The **McGraw-Hill** Companies

Wild & Wacky Science Experiments

Contents

Introduction

What do you call someone who can bend bones in his or her bare hands or change a foul-smelling liquid from putrid purple to putrescent pink with a drop of acid? A scientist, of course!

If these activities sound like your cup of goo, this collection of slippery, slimy, freaky, and fun experiments is for you. They are guaranteed to offend the senses while demonstrating cool science principles.

The experiments in this book are grouped by the type of science they demonstrate. Once you perform each test, read how it worked in the "Action, Reaction, Results" section at the end of the experiment. Boldface words are defined in the glossary at the back of the book.

You should perform each experiment in this book by following the scientific method. The scientific method is the way scientists learn and study the world around them. The following is a list of steps in the scientific method:

- Identify the problem.
- Gather data.
- Form a hypothesis.
- Perform an experiment.
- Analyze the data.
- Draw a conclusion.

The experiments in this book are worthy of an eerie hilltop laboratory, but most can be performed in a small amount of space with ingredients you probably have around the house.

Before you put on your mad-scientist lab coat, read these important safety procedures!

- Before beginning, read the instructions and get an adult's permission.
- If you need to use heat or sharp objects in the test, be sure to ask an adult to give you a hand.
- Never taste anything unless the instructions specifically say it's okay.
- Clean up everything when you are finished, and be sure to wash your hands before and after each experiment.

Ready to begin? If you have a strong stomach, you'll love doing these experiments! If you're squeamish, that's okay. Science isn't always pretty!

To Spill or Not to Spill

Surprise your friends at lunchtime with this experiment. Just be sure to move fast as you demonstrate the properties of polymers, or your performance will be all wet!

Materials

- self-sealing sandwich bag
- water
- sharpened pencil

Directions

❶ Fill the plastic bag with water and seal it.

❷ Hold the bag in front of you. As quickly as you can, stab the pencil through one side of the bag and out the other (speed is very important).

Action, Reaction, Results

Some types of molecules form long chains called polymers. Some polymers are found in natural substances, such as rubber and starch, whereas others are in manufactured goods, such as most plastics. Polyethylene (a type of plastic made from polymers) has a unique property—it shrinks when ripped or when a hole is stabbed in it. When you stab the pencil through the plastic bag, it tightens around the pencil to seal the hole.

Magic Mud

Some substances don't dissolve in water; instead, they do something very interesting. Try the experiment below to create a suspension.

Materials

- 4-ounce bottle of white glue
- $1\frac{1}{2}$ cups distilled water
- two medium glass bowls
- two spoons
- 1 teaspoon borax powder

Directions

❶ Mix the entire bottle of glue and $\frac{1}{2}$ cup distilled water in one bowl. Stir with a spoon.

❷ Pour 1 cup distilled water and 1 teaspoon borax powder into the second bowl. Stir well with the second spoon.

❸ Pour the glue mixture into the borax mixture and stir until you have a thick blob.

❹ Lift the mixture out of the bowl and knead it with your hands until it feels like dough. Try ripping it, pulling it apart slowly, and even bouncing it.

Action, Reaction, Results

The white glue is made up of polymers that become suspended in water. Before you mix the glue with anything else, these polymers tend to slide over each other. Adding borax to the glue causes the polymers to stop moving and form a sort of meshwork instead. The result is a concentrated suspension—liquid water with lots of tiny solid particles (in this case, the polymers) suspended in it. The solid particles do not fit into the spaces between the water molecules, so they can't dissolve in the liquid.

Them Bones!

Your friends and family will be amazed when they see you tying a bone in knots.

Materials

- drumstick or wishbone from a chicken
- scrub brush
- glass jar with a lid, large enough to hold the bone
- white vinegar

Directions

❶ After a nice chicken dinner, save the bone you want to use for your experiment. With the scrub brush, carefully clean all the meat and gristle from the bone and allow it to dry for a few hours.

❷ Fill the jar with vinegar, drop the bone in, and put on the lid. Leave the jar undisturbed for 3 days.

❸ Remove the bone from the vinegar and rinse it with water. It should be soft and rubbery enough to tie in a knot. If it isn't, prepare a fresh jar of vinegar and leave the bone in it for another day or two.

Action, Reaction, Results

Two main elements make up bone. Collagen is a protein that makes bones strong and resilient. Without it, they become very brittle. Apatite is a mineral that makes bones hard. The vinegar is a weak acid that dissolves the apatite in the bone but leaves behind the rubbery collagen.

Something Extra
The strongest bone in the human body is the femur, or thigh bone. It can support more weight than a rod of equal size made of solid steel.

Naked Egg

Have you ever peeled an egg . . . a raw egg, that is? There's a delightfully slimy surprise inside.

Materials

- raw egg
- glass jar with lid
- white vinegar

Directions

❶ Put the egg in the jar, being very careful not to crack the shell.

❷ Fill the jar with enough vinegar to completely cover the egg. Put on the lid and leave the jar undisturbed for about 3 days.

❸ If you check once in a while, you'll see lots of tiny bubbles on the eggshell. When few bubbles are left and the shell is dissolved, very gently pour the vinegar out over the sink so you can catch the egg. Hold it very carefully and observe. It feels soft and slippery. Don't squeeze it or the egg will break.

❹ Hold it up to a light. You can easily see the yolk inside. If you want to save the egg for a while, refill the jar with water, slip the egg in, and replace the lid. It will keep well in the refrigerator for a few days.

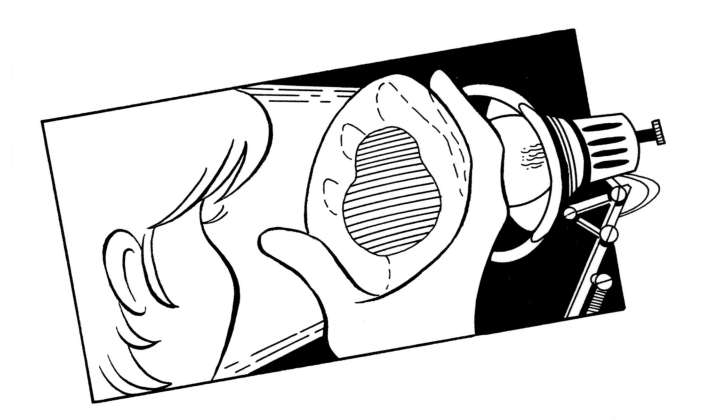

Action, Reaction, Results

The eggshell is made up of a material called *calcium carbonate*. The vinegar reacts with the shell, dissolving it and producing tiny bubbles of carbon dioxide gas. Just inside the egg is a thin membrane that does not react to the vinegar. The membrane keeps the egg intact. Within is the yolk, which is meant to be the food supply for a developing embryo. This is surrounded by the egg white, or albumen, which helps cushion the embryo.

Something Extra

If you store your shell-less egg in water, it will swell because of osmosis. (See page 66, Bloated Raisin Bugs, for an osmosis experiment.) Water moves through the egg membrane, but the molecules that make up the goopy material inside the egg are too big to go the other way. That's called semipermeability.

To see the opposite reaction, place the shell-less, raw egg in a jar of sticky corn syrup. There is more water in the egg than in the corn syrup, so the water molecules will leave the egg. The egg will shrivel into a gooey, yucky mess . . . er, mass.

On the High Seas

Have you ever noticed that oil and water don't mix? That's because they are immiscible (im-MIS-ih-bul) liquids. Check it out.

Materials

- water
- empty soda bottle with cap, label removed (use 1-liter or 2-liter size)
- blue food coloring
- bottle of baby oil

Directions

❶ Pour water into the soda bottle until it is about three-quarters full. Add 5 to 10 drops of blue food coloring to the water and screw the cap on. Shake to mix.

❷ Unscrew the cap. Fill the bottle to the rim with baby oil, then put the cap back on.

❸ Hold the bottle on its side and gently tip it up and down. The colored water will look like the waves of the ocean.

Action, Reaction, Results

This experiment is a demonstration of immiscible liquids—those liquids that are different from each other and will not mix together. As long as you move the bottle gently, the water and baby oil will stay separated.

Something Extra
Create a little sparkle by adding a teaspoon of glitter to the colored water in the bottle.

Morbid Bleeding Blobs

These drippy spheres are guaranteed to make you gasp. What makes them bob? How do they bleed?

Materials

- empty baby-food jar
- rubbing alcohol
- water
- measuring spoons
- mixing spoon
- vegetable oil
- small paper cup
- eyedropper
- red food coloring
- paper towels

Directions

❶ Fill the jar halfway with rubbing alcohol. Add 5 teaspoons of water. Stir the mixture with a spoon, then set the jar aside and wait for the liquid to stop moving.

❷ Meanwhile, place 4 teaspoons of vegetable oil into the paper cup. Add 2 drops of red food coloring, then use the eyedropper to quickly stir the food coloring into the oil. The food coloring stays separated from the oil in tiny balls. Keep mixing and the oil, as it turns blood-red, will look like it blends completely with the food coloring.

❸ Fill the eyedropper with the food coloring and oil mixture. Carefully lower the eyedropper into the jar of alcohol and water solution and place the tip just below the surface. Squeeze the end of the dropper to release a blob of colored oil. Take the eyedropper out of the jar and squeeze out the extra oil onto a paper towel. Refill the eyedropper with more colored oil and repeat the process until you have three or four blobs in the jar.

❹ Watch the result. Your goal is to have the blobs floating in the middle of the jar. But your blood-red blobs will probably do one of two things:

- They will sink. (If they settle at the bottom of the jar, you can add more water, a teaspoon at a time, to make the blobs rise.)

- They will float. (If they rise to the top, you can add more alcohol, a teaspoon at a time, to make the blobs sink.)

Once in a great while, one kid in about 8 million will mix the alcohol and water perfectly on the first try, making the red blobs settle in the middle of the jar. For the rest of you, as you patiently add water or alcohol, teaspoon by teaspoon, watch this process from the side of the jar. Don't place your face near the top of the jar—it puts you in contact with harmful fumes.

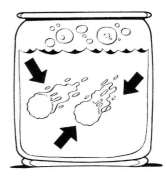

❺ When the blobs are in position, put the lid back on the jar. Peer carefully at the blobs. How do they stay where they are? Why do they look like they're bleeding?

Important! *Once you've finished admiring your bleeding blobs, immediately pour the liquid down the sink, then run tap water for a minute or two. Do not leave it standing around where anyone, especially small children, can get to it. Rubbing alcohol is highly* **toxic** *if swallowed.*

Action, Reaction, Results

There are a couple of things going on in this experiment. The first is a demonstration of **density**, the ratio of weight to **volume** in an object or substance. The oil-based blobs bob in the middle of the jar because the alcohol and water mixture is lighter than water yet heavier than alcohol. In a perfectly mixed **solution**, the blobs are somewhere in between, density-wise—they neither sink to the bottom nor float to the top of the jar.

This experiment is also an example of **immiscible liquids**, or liquids that do not mix together. The oil stays in a round blob because it won't mix with water or alcohol. The blob "bleeds" because the food coloring mixes better with water and alcohol than it does with oil, making food coloring and oil immiscible liquids, too.

Something Extra

There is an old saying that oil and water do not mix. In science lingo, they are immiscible liquids, and there have been many tragic examples of this in the earth's oceans. Anyone who has seen or smelled an oil slick knows just how disgusting it can be. Oil from shipping accidents floats on top of ocean water and eventually makes its way toward the shore, where it leaves an ugly black sludge. To clean up an oil slick, some countries use a chemical spray that makes the oil sink deeper in the water, keeping it away from shore. Others clean up an oil slick by spraying detergent, which breaks up the oil into smaller particles that are then more readily broken up by ocean **microorganisms**.

Perfect Pulse

Your heart pumps blood throughout your entire body. You can tell how many times it pumps each minute by taking your pulse.

Materials

- pea-sized ball of clay
- toothpick

Directions

❶ Place your hand palm side up on a flat surface. Press the ball of clay onto your wrist about an inch below the base of your thumb.

❷ Insert the toothpick into the clay so that it stands upright. Observe carefully as the toothpick twitches slightly back and forth. If it doesn't move, shift the clay until you see the toothpick twitch.

❸ Count the number of twitches that occur in 15 seconds, then multiply that number by four.

❹ Remove the clay and toothpick. Run in place for a minute. Repeat steps 1, 2, and 3. Is there a difference in your heart rate?

Action, Reaction, Results

Your heart beats a certain number of times each minute. Everyone's heartbeat is different, but children average between 80 and 130 heartbeats per minute at rest. With each beat, your heart pumps blood throughout your body. You can feel your pulse as each wave of blood passes through the blood vessel located just below the skin of your wrist. This movement causes the toothpick on your wrist to twitch. Exercise raises the rate of your heartbeat. Your heart beats faster in order to pump blood to all of the hard-working muscles in your body. The toothpick on your wrist probably twitches more often after you exercise.

The See-Through Hand

You can't always believe what you see. Sometimes your eyes play tricks on you. These are known as optical illusions.

Materials

- sheet of construction paper
- tape

Directions

❶ Roll the paper into a tube big enough to look through comfortably with one eye. Tape the paper so that it will not unravel.

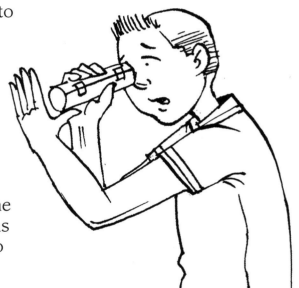

❷ Look through the tube with your right eye. Keep your left eye open and look straight ahead. Place your left hand against the far end of the tube, with the palm facing you. Move your hand slowly a few inches from the end of the tube. Stare straight ahead as you do this, not at your hand. What do you see?

Action, Reaction, Results

Both of your eyes face forward, so your field of vision overlaps. This is called binocular vision. The brain tries to blend what each eye sees into one image. In this case, the left eye sees the hand and the right eye sees the hole. The brain perceives this as a hand with a hole in it.

Something Extra

Hold your index fingers in front of your eyes. Point your fingers at each other but leave an inch-wide gap between them. Keep both eyes open. After a minute you will see a tiny "fingertip" in between your real fingers.

Criss-Cross

Your brain is your center of intelligence. But even the brain can be fooled sometimes.

Materials

- one marble

Directions

❶ Place the marble on a flat surface.

❷ Cross your middle and index fingers.

❸ Close your eyes and gently roll the marble back and forth. Be sure that you touch the marble with the tips of both fingers.

Action, Reaction, Results

You understand the world through your senses. The nerve endings in your fingertips send messages to your brain. By crossing your fingers, you confuse your brain, and it interprets the feeling as two marbles rather than one.

Something Extra
Ask a friend to close his or her eyes and cross his or her fingers. Place five or six marbles on a small, flat plate. Ask your friend to roll them around and try to figure out how many marbles there are.

What a Kick

Believe it or not, what your feet are doing can have an effect on your ability to write!

Materials

- straight-backed chair
- table
- pencil and paper
- an observer

Directions

❶ Sit up straight in the chair, near enough to the table to write. Using the pencil and paper, write the sentence *A quick black cat jumped over the brick wall.*

❷ Lift your right leg up off the floor and begin to turn it in wide circles from right to left.

❸ Try to write the sentence again while moving your leg. Ask your observer to be sure that your leg keeps going in a circular pattern. Can you write the sentence as easily as you did the first time?

Action, Reaction, Results

Your actions are governed by your brain. It takes concentration to move your leg in a circular motion and to write a sentence. When you focus on one, you lose control of the other. It is possible to do both at the same time, but it takes a lot of practice.

At the Center

Do people have a center of gravity?

Materials

- Handkerchief

Directions

❶ Stand in the middle of the room. Drop the handkerchief in front of you. Without bending your knees, lean over and pick up the handkerchief.

❷ Stand with your back against a wall and try the experiment again. Is it harder this time? Do you lose your balance? Why?

❸ Stand in the center of the room and lift your left foot out to the side. Does your body tip slightly to the right to adjust?

❹ Try to do the same thing while standing with your right shoulder and foot against a wall. Can you lift your foot now?

Action, Reaction, Results

People have a center of gravity, too. When you are standing still, you are balanced over your center of gravity. If you move a part of your body, without thinking about it, you automatically make other movements to adjust to the new center. When you bend over to pick up the handkerchief, you also shift your weight back a little to stay in balance. With your back against the wall you cannot shift your weight and so you lose your balance.

Heavy Water

Which has greater density—salt water or fresh water? Here's a way to find out, but you may need a helper to get it right.

Materials

- two empty 2-liter soda bottles with no caps
- water at room temperature
- 6 teaspoons salt
- red food coloring
- 3- by 5-inch card
- duct tape

Directions

❶ Fill both bottles with water.

❷ Add the salt and 10 drops of red food coloring to the first bottle only. Cover the top with your hand, then shake the bottle to mix the contents.

❸ Place the 3- by 5-inch card over the top of the first bottle. Hold the card in place with one hand and flip the bottle over.

❹ You may need help with this step. Balance the opening of the first bottle directly over the opening of the second bottle. When the bottles are as close to each other as possible, slip the card out. Adjust the bottles quickly so the water doesn't spill. Wrap duct tape around the necks of the bottles to prevent leaks.

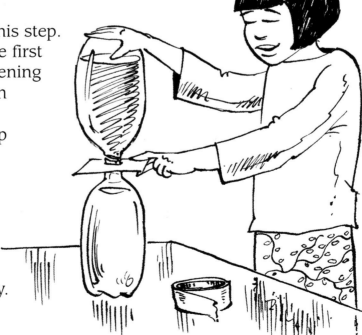

❺ Watch the bottles carefully. What happens to the colored water?

Action, Reaction, Results

The volume, or amount, of water in each bottle is the same. If the density of water in each bottle was also the same—for instance, if the water in both bottles was room-temperature fresh water—then all the water would weigh the same and it would not shift around. In this experiment you use fresh water and salt water. Salt water is more dense than fresh water because of the salt, therefore it is also heavier. The colored salt water sinks to the bottom.

Something Extra
How could you adapt this experiment to test whether cold or warm water is more dense? Try out your idea to see if it works.

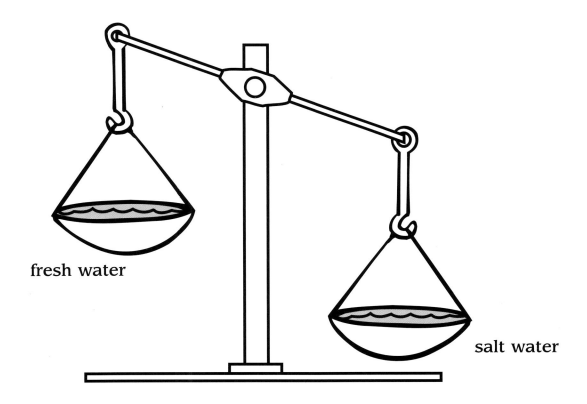

fresh water

salt water

Here Comes the Sludge

Whip up some strange behavior in a bowl. What does it do? Find out . . . if you have the nerve.

Materials

- mixing spoon
- 4-ounce bottle of white glue
- measuring cups
- 1 pint distilled water
- 2 medium-sized glass bowls
- food coloring, any color, or mix up a particularly gross yellow-green
- 1 teaspoon borax powder

Directions

❶ With a spoon, mix the contents of the bottle of glue and $\frac{1}{2}$ cup distilled water in one bowl. Add 5 drops of food coloring and stir well.

❷ Pour 1 cup of distilled water and the borax powder in the second bowl. Stir well.

❸ Pour the glue mixture into the borax mixture and keep stirring until you have a thick glob. Lift it out of the bowl and knead the mixture until it feels like dough. The behavior of the sludge depends on what you do to it, so get creative! Rip the sludge in two. Find out what happens when you pull it slowly. Will it bounce?

Action, Reaction, Results

This is another slippery, slimy example of a non-Newtonian fluid. It is a concentrated suspension. That means it's a liquid with lots of tiny, solid particles suspended in it. The solid particles do not dissolve in the liquid. In fact, they can be removed by passing the liquid through a filter. You can try this yourself using a pint-sized glass jar and a number four coffee filter. Simply place the filter in the top of the jar and slowly pour the liquid into it. The solid material left behind in the filter is called a residue.

Along Came a Spider

Little Miss Muffet wasn't crazy about arachnids, but she loved curds and whey. Here's how to whip up a batch for yourself while demonstrating a chemical reaction called protein coagulation.

Materials

- 1 quart skim milk (1%, 2%, and whole milk also work)
- saucepan
- mixing spoon
- 2 tablespoons lemon juice
- colander or sieve
- cheesecloth

Directions

❶ Pour the milk into the saucepan. With an adult's help, stir constantly over medium heat, bringing it to a slow boil. Keep a close watch on it because milk can boil over quite suddenly.

❷ Have your adult helper remove the pan from the heat and stir in the lemon juice.

❸ Return the pan to the heat and stir the milky mixture until you see lumps. Turn off the heat and let the milk cool to room temperature.

❹ Line the colander or sieve with cheesecloth and put it in the sink. Pour the milk through the colander. The pale fluid running down the drain is called whey. The lumps left behind in the colander are the curds, a simplified version of cottage cheese! It is certainly safe to eat, though you may not find it very tasty.

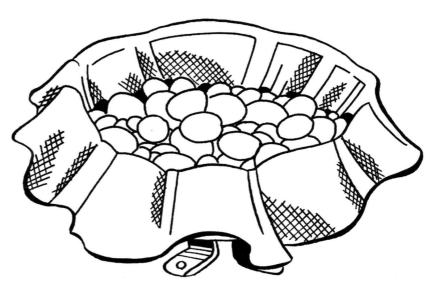

Action, Reaction, Results

When a water-soluble protein, such as that in milk, is heated to a certain temperature, or acid is added, it becomes denatured. (In this experiment both heat and acid are used.) "Denatured" means a change takes place and the protein will no longer remain dissolved in a fluid. It forms clumps, or curds. The acid in the lemon juice causes such a chemical reaction when it comes in contact with protein in the milk. The result is curds and whey. The clumping reaction demonstrates protein coagulation. This is the process used to make cheese, a valuable source of protein in the human diet.

Something Extra

One legend maintains that the first cheese was made by accident. Supposedly an Arabian merchant filled a pouch with milk, then after riding through the desert all day he found that the milk had separated into curds and whey. It was the heat and a substance in the lining of the pouch that caused this reaction. The substance is called rennet, and it is an enzyme, a protein that helps a chemical reaction take place. Like lemon juice, rennet contributes to the milk-curdling reaction in milk. The pouch, by the way, was made out of a sheep's stomach.

Slime Time

Is it a solid or a liquid? This slippery, slimy ooze has a split personality.

Materials

- 1 cup cornstarch
- mixing bowl
- water
- measuring spoons
- mixing spoon

Directions

❶ Put the cornstarch in the bowl. Add water by the teaspoonful and stir. Keep adding teaspoons of water until the mixture is fluid but very hard to stir. It should have the consistency of thick mud.

❷ Reach in and pick up a handful of the gooey fluid. Don't be squeamish— you have to move fast for this to work. Quickly roll the glop between your hands. It will become a firm ball.

❸ Hold your hands over the bowl and stop rolling. The ball becomes fluid again and slippery slime drips through your fingers.

Action, Reaction, Results

Your slime is an example of a non-Newtonian fluid. Fluids have a property called viscosity, or resistance to flow. The British scientist Sir Isaac Newton (1642–1727) is best known for his theories about light, gravity, and motion. He said that the viscosity of a fluid, such as water, can be changed only by raising or lowering its temperature. Sometimes in science you'll find an exception to a rule, and non-Newtonian fluids are the exception to Sir Isaac's rule on viscosity. Non-Newtonian fluids can be changed by temperature or, as shown in this experiment, by applying force. Putting pressure on the slippery slime by rubbing it between your hands makes it resistant to flowing.

Something Extra
Believe it or not, glass is not a solid but rather a very viscous liquid. Adding heat will cause glass to flow. Non-Newtonian fluids, like glass, may also change over time. If you are lucky enough to live near a very old building that has the original glass in its windows, check closely. You may find that the panes are a tiny bit thicker at the bottom. That is because the glass has flowed ever so slightly downward over many years.

Demented Dessert

In an old movie called **The Blob,** *a creature that looked a lot like an oversized lump of gelatin gobbled up a bellyful of townsfolk. Usually it's the other way around—flavored gelatin is a great dessert that kids can really sink their teeth into. It also makes a gooey, oozy example of a rather unusual substance. Try this demonstration, then feel free to eat the evidence.*

Materials

- 1 cup apple juice
- saucepan
- small glass bowl (Pyrex® is recommended)
- 1 packet unflavored gelatin
- mixing spoon
- butter knife
- microwave-safe plate

Directions

❶ Pour the cup of apple juice into the pan and warm it over medium heat until it comes to a boil. Ask an adult to remove the juice from the heat and pour it into a glass bowl.

❷ Sprinkle in the unflavored gelatin. Stir until the powder dissolves, and refrigerate for several hours.

❸ Once the gelatin has set completely, remove it from the bowl in one piece. To do this, place the bowl in warm water for 2 minutes. Then run a butter knife around the edge of the gelatin. Slide the gelatin carefully onto a microwave-safe plate.

❹ Now place the wiggly gelatin in a microwave on medium power for about 30 seconds, then check it. (If you don't have a microwave, you can use an oven heated on its lowest setting. You'll need to substitute an oven-safe plate for a microwave-safe plate.) You should see that the juice has been released and the slippery ooze is seeping across the plate. If your microwave has a clear door, you can even watch as the gelatin begins to "sweat."

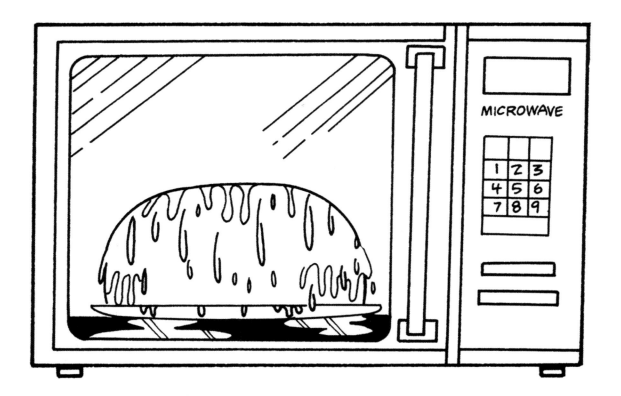

Action, Reaction, Results

Gelatin dessert is a substance known as a *colloid*. A colloid is made up of very tiny particles, called the *solute*, in a liquid, called the *solvent*. If the solute is solid and the solvent is liquid, then the colloid is known as a *sol* (such as milk and glue). If the solute and the solvent are both liquid, the colloid is called an emulsion (such as mayonnaise).

In this experiment, the colloid is called a *gel*. The solid part is the powdered gelatin—a protein that forms a kind of mesh. When mixed with hot water (or in this case, hot apple juice), gelatin granules absorb the liquid and swell, then melt. As the solution cools and is chilled, the liquid is trapped within the mesh network. The network a colloid forms is broken down by heat. When you put your gelatin in the microwave, the fluid was released because the network trapping it was no longer in place.

Something Extra
Gelatin is a substance that can be made by boiling animal cartilage, hides, skin, and bone in water, then letting the result cool until it sets into a gel.

Water Sculpture

How do stalactites form in caves?

Materials

- 2 glass jars
- spoon
- small plate
- pot holders
- Epsom salts
- 8 inches of heavy wool knitting yarn

Directions

❶ Have a parent help you fill both jars with very hot water. Stir in Epsom salts one spoonful at a time, until the water can hold no more.

❷ Place the jars where they will not be disturbed. Put the small plate between them, and put one end of the wool yarn in each jar. After three or four days, check your experiment. What is happening? What is your stalagmite made of? Will the columns on the bottom and top eventually meet? Try it.

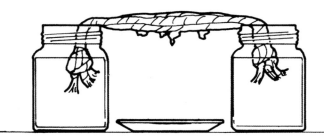

Action, Reaction, Results

The water and dissolved Epsom salts in the jars are absorbed by the wool. As the water collects in the center of the strand, it will begin to drip very slowly. As each drop hangs from the wool, the water begins to evaporate leaving behind the salts, which build up after a while. Some drops may fall to the plate and a salt formation will grow there, too. It is through this same process that cones and columns form in caves. A STALACTITE forms on the roof of a cave. The formation on the floor of a cave is a STALAGMITE.

On Pins and Needles

These crazy crystals really make a point, and the weird, crusty growths seem to appear out of nowhere. How do they form? Why are they shaped the way they are?

Materials

- large jar lid
- pencil
- black construction paper
- scissors
- 4 or 5 tablespoons Epsom salts (available at drugstores and many supermarkets)
- 1 cup lukewarm water
- mixing spoon

Directions

❶ Use the jar lid to draw a circle with a pencil on the construction paper. Cut out the circle and place it inside the jar lid. This will give the lid a dark background, making it easier to observe the crystals.

❷ Add the Epsom salts to the cup of lukewarm water. Stir until the Epsom salts disappear.

❸ Pour about ¼ inch of the salty water from the cup into the lid. Set the lid in a warm place with good air circulation, but not in direct sunlight. Leave it undisturbed for at least 24 hours. Long, thin, needlelike crystals will develop on the lid.

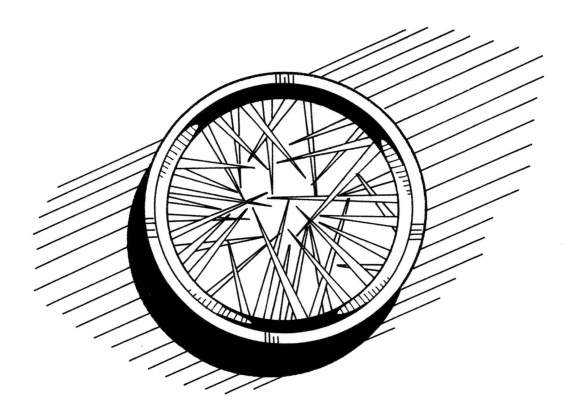

Something Extra

For more than 300 years people have relied on a hot bath with Epsom salts to ease sore muscles. This common mineral is also known as epsomite, and it is often found as a scabby crust in mines and caves. The pure quality used in medicinal Epsom salts is named for a town called Epsom, in Surrey, England. There, evaporated mineral waters left behind huge deposits of the crystals, making the place a gigantic version of the experiment you just performed.

Action, Reaction, Results

A crystal is a basic form of a solid substance in which the **molecules** are arranged in a regular, geometric pattern. When solid substances are pure (made up of a single kind of molecule), they usually have a definite crystal form that has flat surfaces that always meet at the same angle.

The Epsom salts used in this experiment were crystals before they were ground into a grainy powder. When the powdered Epsom salts dissolve in water, they form a solution in which the salt molecules are randomly scattered. As the water **evaporates**, it leaves the salt behind. The salt molecules return to their natural orderly pattern, forming thin crystals. That is the way they looked before being crushed into grainy Epsom salts. The formation of crystals is called *crystallization*.

Something Extra

There are many salt lakes in the world—bodies of water so high in salt content that as the lake waters evaporate, salt crystals are left behind on the shoreline. One very awesome salt lake is Mono Lake. Located in California, it is three times as salty as the Atlantic Ocean. It is also loaded with sodium carbonate, a close cousin to baking soda. This unique combination supports a growth of blue-green algae that acts as food for an outrageously gross population of brine flies. At the end of the summer some 4,000 flies crowd each square foot of salt-encrusted shoreline! In the late 1800s that meant good eating for members of the native Paiute tribe. They gathered and ate the larva and pupa forms of the fly, which are yellowish and oily but very nutritious.

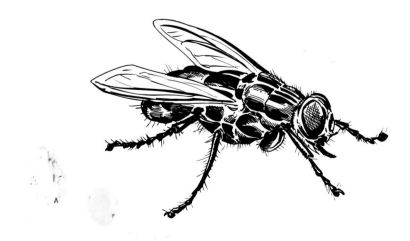

Crystals

How do crystals form?

Materials

- tall glass jar
- spoon
- sugar
- food coloring
- paper clip
- pencil
- 1 foot of light string

Directions

❶ Fill the jar with very hot water. Stir in sugar, a spoonful at a time, until no more will dissolve in the water. Add a few drops of food coloring.

❷ Tie one end of the string around the middle of the pencil and attach the paper clip to the other end. Lower the string into the jar. Turn the pencil to shorten the string until the paper clip hangs an inch from the bottom.

❸ Let the jar set for a few days. Crystals will form. The longer you wait, the larger the crystals will grow. Are the crystals made of sugar? Taste them. This is how rock candy is made. Crystals can be made from salt, too.

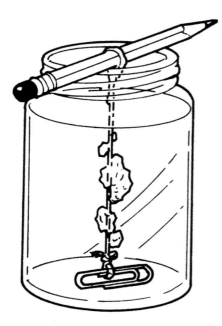

Action, Reaction, Results

When certain substances form, the atoms become arranged in   orderly pattern. This pattern is the CRYSTAL STRUCTURE. As more atoms are   acted and join this structure, the crystal "grows." Crystals form in one of tv   .ays, evaporation or cooling. By stirring the sugar into hot water you break down the crystals. As the water cools, the crystals reform.

Permanent Ice

Why don't the polar ice caps melt away?

Materials

- black paint
- white paint
- paintbrush
- 2 coffee cans
- thermometer

Directions

❶ Paint the outside of one can black, the other white. Fill both cans with water.

❷ Place both cans in the sun and record the temperature of the water. An hour later, which can do you think will contain hotter water?

❸ Test it. Which one was hotter? Bright surfaces reflect heat while dark surfaces absorb it. Would a field of bright snow absorb or reflect the warm rays of the sun?

Action, Reaction, Results

The rate at which a surface reflects light is called its ALBEDO. Dark surfaces have a low albedo while bright snow has a very high albedo. Instead of being absorbed, much of the heat radiation that can cause the temperature to rise is reflected away. The longer the ice field, the greater this effect becomes. Of course, some of the ice and snow melts and the ice caps become smaller in summer, but they never melt away completely.

What Goes Up Must Come Down

What is the rain cycle?

Materials

- 3 small potted plants
- 2 metal cookie trays
- hot plate
- teakettle
- padded glove
- 12 ice cubes

Directions

❶ Place the plants on one tray next to the hot plate. Fill the teakettle with water, place it on the hot plate, and bring it to a boil with the spout facing toward the tray.

❷ Fill the second tray with ice and some water. Hold it above the plants and close enough to the teakettle so that vapor will reach it.

❸ The teakettle represents the source of the water vapor, such as an ocean or lake. The upper tray is cold air in the atmosphere. What will happen as the water vapor condenses? What will finally happen to the water that has fallen on the small plants as rain?

Action, Reaction, Results

Water is constantly evaporating from the surface of Earth's great bodies of water. The water vapor is carried by warm air high into the upper atmosphere. At this point, the air cools, the water vapor condenses, and, when conditions are right, it falls as rain. Some of the rainwater may be absorbed by plants and released back into the air through transpiration. (Transpiration is the passage of water vapor from a living body.) Most of it finds its way to streams, rivers, lakes, and oceans, and the cycle begins again.

Fog in a Bottle

How does fog form?

Materials

- 1 ice cube
- plastic wrap
- potholders
- clear glass pop or juice bottle

Directions

❶ Using the potholders, fill the bottle with hot water. Let it set for a moment. Pour out most of the water leaving about an inch in the bottle.

❷ Put the ice cube on top of the bottle. What happens as the warm, moist air meets the cold air?

❸ Cover the ice in plastic wrap and repeat the experiment. Did the fog appear? Is the water vapor from which the fog forms in the ice or in the warm air?

Action, Reaction, Results

The warm air in the bottle holds water vapor. It is cooled when it comes in contact with the ice. The water vapor condenses onto particles in the air, forming tiny droplets that you see as fog.

Sticky Weather

Why are hot, humid days more uncomfortable than hot, dry days?

Materials

- glass
- paper towels
- thermometer
- twist tie
- blotting paper

Directions

❶ Fill the glass with water that is the same temperature as the room. Tear a small strip from the paper towel, dip it in the water, and wrap it around the bulb of the thermometer. Hold the strip in place with the twist tie. Record the temperature. Has it changed?

❷ Put the thermometer in the glass of water and record the temperature after five minutes.

❸ Line the glass with a piece of blotting paper. Wait a moment, then pour out the water. In the air of the room, wrapping the thermometer in a moist towel made the temperature drop. Will the same thing happen in the moisture-filled air in the glass? Try it.

Action, Reaction, Results

Water vapor in the air is called HUMIDITY. The evaporation of water from your skin as sweat has a cooling effect, but the air can only hold a certain amount of water. When humidity is high sweat will stay on your skin and you will feel sticky and uncomfortable.

Groaning Glass

These grating sound effects can set your teeth on edge. Try it with glasses of different sizes, and you can start your own creepy chorus.

Materials

- stem wineglass (the thinner the glass the better)
- dishwashing liquid
- water
- dishtowel
- white vinegar
- small bowl

Directions

❶ Wash the glass and your hands in warm, soapy water to get rid of any grease or oil. Dry thoroughly.

❷ Holding it by the stem, place the squeaky-clean glass on a flat surface. Pour a little vinegar into the bowl (you won't need more than $\frac{1}{4}$ cup) and dip the index finger of your free hand in the vinegar.

❸ Holding the glass at its base, rub your wet finger around the rim of the glass until you hear a high-pitched whine.

Action, Reaction, Results

Washing everything well and using vinegar rids the glass and your finger of any oil or **lubricant**. As you rub, you create **friction** between the rim of the glass and your finger. Friction is the resistance to motion between two surfaces moving across each other. This resistance causes the glass and surrounding air to vibrate, which you hear as a whining sound. The pitch of the sound is determined by the frequency or number of vibrations per second. The higher the frequency, the higher the pitch.

Something Extra
The friction between your finger and the glass results in the sound you hear in this experiment. Another product of friction is heat. To feel heat from friction, try rubbing your dry hands together very fast. Do they warm up?

Dancing Coin

Here's a way to make a coin jump without even touching it. It isn't magic, it's a demonstration of the effect of gas expansion.

Materials

- empty 2-liter soda bottle with no cap
- freezer
- quarter
- water

Directions

❶ Put the empty, open soda bottle in the freezer for about 10 minutes.

❷ Dip the quarter in water.

❸ Take the bottle out of the freezer and set it on a flat surface in a sunny spot. Quickly cover the open mouth of the bottle with the wet coin. The coin will soon start to tap up and down. As long as the coin is centered over the opening of the bottle, the tapping will continue.

Action, Reaction, Results

By putting the bottle in the freezer, you chill the air that is inside the bottle. The cold air contracts, which means it takes up less space. When you take the bottle out of the freezer, the air inside warms and expands but is trapped by the wet coin. The wetness helps to create a seal that keeps the air inside the bottle. As the air slowly pushes upward, it builds up enough pressure to lift the coin and escape in a short burst. The pressure must build again before another burst of air can escape. The coin jumps slightly each time the air escapes.

The Egg and I

Can a change in air pressure create a pulling force?

Materials

- 1 small hard-boiled egg
- cooking oil
- baby's milk bottle
- matches
- small piece of paper folded like an accordion

Directions

❶ Peel the egg. Rub a little cooking oil on the rim of the bottle.

❷ Ask your adult helper to light the paper with a match and drop it into the bottle.

❸ Quickly place the egg on top of the bottle. The gas inside will expand and be forced out of the bottle because the egg is not an airtight stopper. What do you think will happen when the air inside the bottle begins to cool? Is the egg pulled into the bottle? How can you get it out?

❹ Tip the bottle upside down, push the egg aside, and blow into the bottle as hard as you can. Now hold out your hand and the egg will pop out onto it.

Action, Reaction, Results

The heated air in the bottle expands and much of it is forced out. As the bottle cools, there is less air within and so the pressure is lower inside the bottle than outside. Since the egg is not a perfect seal, outside air is drawn into the bottle and the egg is sucked in along with it. By blowing into the bottle you increase the air pressure inside. There is no longer room for the egg, so it pops out again.

The Crusher

What could be better than bending steel with your bare hands? How about destroying a bottle with a sickening crunch from 10 feet away?

Materials

- approximately ½ cup warm tap water
- 1-liter plastic soda bottle with cap
- 10 ice cubes
- plastic bag
- small hammer or mallet

Directions

❶ Pour the warm water in the bottle, then immediately screw on the cap and set aside.

❷ Place the ice cubes in the plastic bag and crush them into chilling chunks with the hammer or mallet.

❸ Pour the water out of the bottle into the sink, add the little ice chunks, then screw the cap back on tightly. Shake the bottle, then place it on a table where it will not be disturbed. (Don't put it in sunlight.) Now sit back and watch! It might take as little as 10 minutes before you hear the first crunch; then slowly, over the next several minutes, the bottle will cave in on itself, popping and groaning all the while!

Action, Reaction, Results

Air pressure is the pressure that air in the atmosphere exerts on everything it touches. It is created by the weight of air above the earth's surface.

Empty plastic bottles don't usually collapse when they are just sitting around because the pressure inside and outside the bottle is equal. In other words, the air inside the bottle pushes outward as hard as the outside air pushes in. In this experiment you first warm the air in the bottle to cause it to expand, then you chill it rapidly. As the warm air in the bottle cools, it **contracts**, or shrinks. It takes up less space, so the air pressure on the inside of the bottle is lower than the outside air pressure. The higher pressure on the outside causes the bottle to cave in on itself.

Something Extra

*At sea level and at 32°F, the earth's atmosphere presses down at about 15 pounds per square inch. At this very moment, your body is experiencing this pressure, but you don't collapse inward because the air and **fluids** inside of you push outward (or expand) until the forces pushing out and the forces pushing in are equal.*

That's okay if you are on this planet, but it could pose a problem if you were in outer space. On a space walk an astronaut has to wear a pressurized suit to keep from blowing up like a balloon. Without a pressurized suit, not only would the space traveler have nothing to breathe, but the air and fluids in his or her body would keep expanding until the space traveler's eyeballs popped out and his or her skin and other organs ruptured.

Surprising Rising Ball

How does matter respond to its environment? This experiment demonstrates a characteristic, or property, of matter.

Materials

- 2 cups uncooked rice
- quart jar with lid
- large marble or ping-pong ball

Directions

❶ Pour the rice into the jar.

❷ Place the marble or ping-pong ball on top of the rice. Fasten the lid onto the jar, then turn the jar over.

❸ Using one hand, shake the jar hard from side to side. As you are shaking it, the marble or ball will rise to the surface.

Action, Reaction, Results

The rice may fill part of the jar, but something else is between each grain—empty space. When you shake the jar, the rice grains tumble over each other, filling in the empty spaces. The marble or ball is too big to fill in any of these spaces, so it moves upward. This experiment demonstrates a property of matter: No two objects can occupy the same place at the same time.

Expand or Contract

What happens when a gas becomes hotter?

Materials

- nail
- food coloring
- clay
- container large enough to hold the bottle
- bottle with a plastic screw-on cap
- drinking straw

Directions

❶ With the nail, make a hole in the bottle cap large enough for the straw to fit through. Fill the bottle halfway with water and add a few drops of food coloring.

❷ Screw on the cap, and slide the straw until it is about an inch from the bottom of the bottle. Seal around the cap's edges with clay and plug the hole of the straw too, but make a small hole in the center of the clay with the nail. Do you think you can get the water out of the bottle without tipping it over or taking off the cap?

❸ Place the container in the sink because this can be a little messy. Fill the container with very hot water and put the bottle in it. Wait until the air in the bottle warms up. What happens?

Action, Reaction, Results

Most things expand or get larger when they heat up. As the warm air in the bottle expanded, it pushed down on the water. This caused some of the water to travel up the straw and spray out of the top of the bottle.

The Big Story

Do solids expand when heated?

Materials

- 1 piece of wood about 8 inches long, 6 inches wide, and $\frac{1}{2}$ inch thick (piece A)
- 2 pieces of wood about 4 x 4 inches and $\frac{1}{2}$ inch thick (pieces B and C)
- aluminum rod about 1 foot long
- crayon, pen or pencil
- 3 candles
- nails

Directions

❶ Ask your adult helper to drill a hole in one of the smaller pieces of wood (piece B); then nail the three pieces together as in the illustration, with piece A on the bottom.

❷ Fit the aluminum rod into the hole in piece B. Rest the end on a nail driven into piece C. Make a mark on the wood at the end of the rod.

❸ Measure the distance between piece A and the rod. Cut the candles one inch shorter than this distance. Place the three candles under the metal rod and light them.

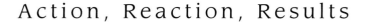

❹ After a few minutes, compare the end of the rod with your mark. Is the rod longer? Did the heat from the candles cause it to expand? Make a new mark at the end of the rod and remove the candles.

❺ After the metal has cooled completely, check the mark again. What happened?

Action, Reaction, Results

When most materials are heated, the atoms that they are made of move farther apart. This causes the material to expand.

Which Way Worms

Like all living things, worms have ways to sense the world around them. Try this test of a worm's ability to detect odors.

Remember: *The worms are your partners in this experiment and should never be harmed.*

Materials

- paper towel
- water
- earthworms
- tweezers
- cotton balls
- nail polish remover

Directions

❶ Dampen a paper towel with water and place some earthworms on it to crawl around.

❷ Use the tweezers to drench a cotton ball in nail polish remover and put it near but not touching a worm's head. The end closest to the wide band on a worm's body is the head.

❸ Observe the direction in which the worm crawls. Be careful not to actually touch any of the worms. Release the worms into their natural environment when the experiment is over.

Action, Reaction, Results

Even though you don't touch the worm, it moves away from the cotton ball. An earthworm doesn't have a nose. What it does have is a nerve cord that extends the length of its body, and masses of nerve tissue in each segment. This enables it to detect an unpleasant odor and change its direction.

Something Extra
Will a worm be attracted to some odors and repulsed by others? Try using different scents such as vanilla, squashed banana, and bleach.

Maggot Magic

Does rotting meat turn into maggots? If rotting meat is left outside in hot weather, newly hatched flies, called maggots, soon appear in the meat. The wormlike maggots eventually grow into adult flies. The appearance of maggots in rotting meat led some ancient people to believe that rotting meat turns into maggots.

Materials

- two plastic cups
- hole punch
- scissors
- string
- two small pieces of raw meat
- small piece of cloth
- rubber band

Directions

❶ Get two plastic cups. Use a hole punch to make two holes near the rim of each cup, one on each side.

❷ Use the scissors to cut four pieces of string, each about 3 feet long. Tie the ends of the strings to the holes in the cups, one string per hole.

❸ Put a small piece of raw meat in each cup.

❹ Leave one cup uncovered. Cover the top of the other cup with a small piece of cloth. Fasten the cloth tightly with a rubber band. Put tape over the string holes in this cup, so that insects can't get in.

❺ Find a tree with a high, long branch. Ask an adult to help you tie both cups to the tree branch, high enough to be out of reach of dogs, cats, and other animals.

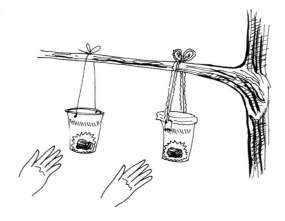

6 Ask an adult to help you smear a thick layer of petroleum jelly down the length of each string, to keep out ants.

7 Look in the cups every day until you see maggots. Where are the maggots?

Action, Reaction, Results

Maggots only appeared in the uncovered cup. Flies are attracted to rotting meat, where they lay eggs. However, the flies were able to reach only the meat in the uncovered cup. The fly eggs in the uncovered cup hatched into maggots. This experiment proves that fly eggs, not rotting meat, give rise to maggots. A similar experiment was done over 300 years ago by an Italian scientist named Francesco Redi, who proved that living things don't "hatch" from nonliving substances.

Something Extra

Grow a fruit fungus. Make two holes in a plastic cup and tie strings to the holes, as described above. Place a slice of banana in the cup. Cover the top of the cup with a small piece of cloth, and fasten the cloth tightly with a rubber band. Put tape over the string holes in the cup. Tie the cup to a tree branch, out of reach of animals. Smear petroleum jelly down the length of the strings, to keep out ants. Check the banana slice after a week or two. Is something growing on the banana?

Foul Fruit

Imagine this: You have your taste buds all ready for a yummy apple. You open wide, take a big bite, and . . . disgusting! You get a mouthful of brown, mealy pulp. In this experiment, you will speed up the process of fresh, crisp fruit turning to mush.

Materials

- knife
- ripe apple or banana
- 2 small bowls
- lemon juice
- mixing spoon

Directions

❶ With an adult's help, peel the fruit and cut it into small pieces. Put half in one bowl and set it aside.

❷ Put the other half of the fruit in the second bowl, add the lemon juice, and toss with a spoon until the fruit is coated.

❸ After about 30 minutes, check the fruit in each bowl. The bare fruit should be starting to turn brown. The fruit with the lemon juice should look much fresher.

❹ Leave the fruit undisturbed for 2 more hours, then check again. By this time the bare fruit should be quite brown. If you want to up the grossness quotient of this experiment, let the untreated fruit remain out in the bowl for several days and observe the changes it goes through.

Action, Reaction, Results

Chemicals in the fruit, called **aldehydes**, combine with oxygen in the air causing a **chemical reaction**. A chemical reaction is a change that takes place when two or more substances interact. Here, the aldehydes in the fruit mix with oxygen, turning the bare fruit sickly brown. After several hours it begins to get mushy. The fruit coated with the lemon juice will also turn brown, but much more slowly, because lemon juice is a weak **acid** that delays the process. Such weak acids are called **antioxidants**. Antioxidants are used as preservatives in many foods, paints, and fuels.

Something Extra
You can speed up the browning process dramatically by placing the fruit in a blender and adding about 4 tablespoons of hydrogen peroxide. Blending exposes more of the aldehydes to the air and the peroxide releases oxygen. Once you have watched the show, carefully dispose of the mess. It is not safe to eat! It could make you very sick!

Merry Maggot Menagerie

Who couldn't use a few more friends? Here's a way to raise your own ghastly brood, then watch as they change right before your very eyes. This experiment should be started on a nice spring or summer day when fruit flies are plentiful.

Materials

- overripe fruit, such as a banana or apple
- clean quart jar
- cheesecloth (or one foot cut from a pair of panty hose—no holes in the toes!)
- rubber band
- magnifying glass

Directions

❶ Place the soon-to-be-rotten fruit in the open jar and put it in a safe, shady spot outside where it can sit undisturbed for at least 4 or 5 days.

❷ The day after you start your experiment, check the jar. If you see tiny black fruit flies bouncing around on the fruit, cover the top with a piece of cheesecloth or panty hose and secure with a rubber band. If no fruit flies are spotted, continue checking the jar each day until they appear.

❸ Once you've covered the jar, give the flies 2 days to enjoy their reeking meal and lay eggs. Then release them from the jar.

❹ Re-cover the jar with the cheesecloth or panty hose and store it in a warm place where no people or animals will touch it.

❺ Over the next 2 weeks, check the fruit in the jar every day with a magnifying glass without removing the cloth covering. With luck, you'll see a colony of fruit flies form and observe their progression from eggs (tiny, grayish specks) to adults.

Action, Reaction, Results

Leaving ripening fruit out is like sounding a dinner bell for adult fruit flies. Not only do they gorge themselves on the sweet pulp, but they lay eggs there, too, to give their young a meal the moment they hatch. Like many other insects, fruit flies go through four stages of development.

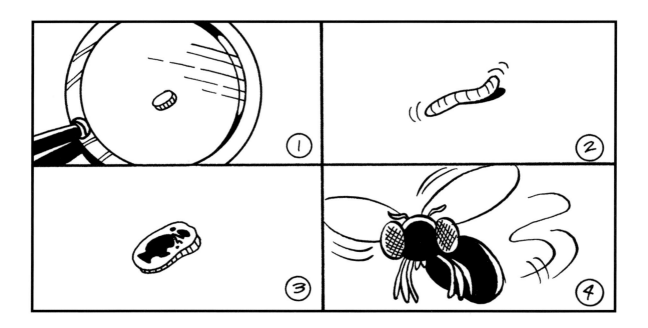

Something Extra

The egg is the first stage. The second stage is the larva, which looks something like a small worm. In the fly, the larva is generally called a maggot. The third, or pupa stage, is a resting stage during which the insect develops its adult features. Finally, during the fourth stage, an adult fly emerges. The entire process is called **metamorphosis**. *Different kinds of insects go through the four stages of metamorphosis at different rates. For example, certain types lay eggs that hatch in hours, while others take days.*

Attack of the Night Crawlers

Believe it or not, you can help the environment by raising a crop of squirmy houseguests that are first-class recyclers. They eat nothing but garbage and leave behind something very useful for the garden: compost. Made up of decayed plant matter, compost is one of the best fertilizers you can find.

Materials

- hammer and nail
- plastic bin with tight-fitting lid (approximately 1 foot x 2 feet x 6 inches)
- base material (grass clippings, finely shredded newspaper, dried leaves)
- water
- 1 cup sand or soil
- approximately 24 earthworms
- scraps of fruit, vegetables, coffee grounds, eggshells, tea bags (Do not use meat or dairy products, or anything with sugar or salt in it.)

Directions

❶ With an adult's help, use the hammer and nail to poke 2 rows of holes in the sides of the container (at least 10 per side). Poke 10 or 12 holes in the bottom, too.

❷ Gather enough base material to fill the container a little more than half full. Dampen the material slightly with water, then, with your hands, mix in a cup of sand or soil. Be sure the material is situated loosely in the container, not packed.

❸ Place about two dozen earthworms, or night crawlers, into the container. (You can dig them up outside, or buy them at a store that sells live bait.) Set the container on blocks or bricks so that air can circulate around it. If you store it outside, find an area that is protected from wind, rain, and direct sunlight. It should also be in an area that won't be disturbed.

❹ Add approximately 2 cups of food scraps by lifting chunks of the base material and slipping scraps within. Put on the lid. As the worms use up the food, you'll need to add more. Each time you do, put the food in a different area of the bin. Gently blend the

scraps into the base material with your hands, being careful not to harm the tenants. Always wash your hands thoroughly after mixing. Repeat this step for 2 months. At that point you should find that much of the material in the bin has been converted into a dark, spongy "soil."

❺ After 2 or 3 months your compost will be ready to use in a garden or in potted plants. Carefully remove the worms and release them in a safe place such as a garden or park, or put them aside while you set up a new batch of material for compost.

Action, Reaction, Results

The earthworm is one of the original recyclers. It eats its own weight in decaying plant matter each day and passes out digested material, creating the world's best natural fertilizer. Another plus: Earthworms aerate the soil and create better drainage.

During the course of this experiment, if you feed your wiggly crew regularly and keep them in a place with good air circulation, the compost won't have anything but a rich, earthy smell. If it's stinky, you are probably giving the worms more scraps than they can handle. By the way, earthworms break down food scraps seven times faster than the material would break down without worms.

Something Extra

Some people are squeamish about handling earthworms. That's easy to understand if you live in Australia. One earthworm species there can grow to 11 feet in length!

Putrid, Pungent Punch

If you can stand the stench, this foul-smelling fluid is a useful acid-testing indicator.

Materials

- knife
- half of a red cabbage
- pot
- 1 quart distilled water
- colander or sieve
- measuring cup
- 3 small glass jars with lids
- label
- marker
- measuring spoons
- 1 tablespoon lemon juice
- $\frac{1}{4}$ teaspoon baking soda

Directions

❶ With an adult's help, cut the cabbage into small, bite-sized pieces and place in a pot. Pour in the distilled water and bring to a full boil. Turn off the heat and allow the fluid to cool. (The smell of this experiment will become apparent here!)

❷ Pour the cooled liquid through a colander into a measuring cup. (You can use the cabbage in your compost heap [see page 56], or eat it with a little butter and salt. It is a good source of vitamins A and C, as well as calcium. Besides, it tastes great.)

❸ The cabbage water will be an inky blue. Pour it into the first glass jar and label it *cabbage indicator*.

❹ Pour about ¼ cup of cabbage indicator into another glass jar, then add the tablespoon of lemon juice. The indicator will turn bright pink in the presence of acid.

❺ Pour about ¼ cup of cabbage indicator into the last glass jar. Add ¼ teaspoon of baking soda. The indicator turns dark green in the presence of a base (a substance that reacts with acid to form a salt).

❻ Using the same process, test other foods to see if you can detect an acid or a base. Coffee, vinegar, and milk are good foods to test.

Action, Reaction, Results

The hot water releases chemicals from the cabbage, some of which appear blue. When the chemicals come in contact with an acid or a **base**, a chemical reaction changes the color of the fluid from blue to pink or green. By carefully watching for any changes in the color of the indicator, you can detect even small amounts of acid or base in the substance you are testing.

Where Did It Go?

You can make matter appear to disappear right before your eyes. It isn't really gone, though. What seems like sleight of hand is really an example of a solution.

Materials

- 1¼ cups water at room temperature
- glass pint jar
- marking pen
- masking tape (optional)
- spoon
- ¼ cup sugar

Directions

❶ Pour ¼ cup water into the jar. Draw a line to mark the water level and label it ¼. If your pen won't work on glass, write on a piece of masking tape and put it on the jar at the right water level. Add another ¼ cup water and mark it ½. Add one more ¼ cup water and label it ¾.

❷ Empty the contents of the jar into the sink. Refill the jar with water to the ½ cup mark.

❸ With a spoon, stir ¼ cup sugar into the water and check the level of the fluid. Do ½ cup water and ¼ cup sugar equal ¾ cup water?

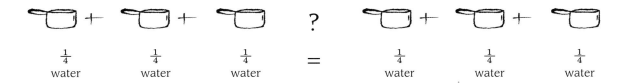

| ¼ water | ¼ water | ¼ water | ? = | ¼ water | ¼ water | ¼ water |

Action, Reaction, Results

In a liquid state, water molecules have plenty of spaces in between them. Many of the sugar molecules simply fill up these spaces without making much of a change in the water level. When the sugar dissolves, or fills in the spaces between the water molecules, a solution is formed. The sugar serves as a solute (the material that dissolves), and the water serves as a solvent (what the material dissolves in).

Ups and Downs

Have you ever taken a sip of soda and felt a tickle at the end of your nose? That's caused by tiny bubbles of carbon dioxide, a gas, which gives soda its fizz. Those bubbles can do more, too. Try this and learn about some properties of gas.

Materials

- glass pint jar
- unopened bottle of club soda
- 10 raisins

Directions

❶ Fill the jar with club soda.

❷ Add the raisins, one at a time, to the club soda, and watch what happens. The raisins will rise, then fall, then eventually rise again.

Action, Reaction, Results

Club soda fizzes because it is filled with carbon dioxide gas. The gas bubbles rise because they are lighter than the liquid they are in. In this experiment the bubbles cling to the raisins and carry them to the surface. When the bubbles break, the raisins sink, until new bubbles attach to the raisins and carry them up again.

Bloated Raisin Bugs

In just a matter of hours, you can turn a handful of innocent raisins into a herd of what look like bloated water bugs. Then you can really freak out your friends by eating one!

Materials

- pint- or quart-sized glass jar
- warm water
- 12 to 15 raisins, any kind

Directions

❶ Fill the glass jar within 2 inches of the top rim with lukewarm tap water.

❷ Drop the raisins into the jar, then place the jar where it can be left undisturbed. Let the experiment sit overnight or for at least 6 hours.

❸ When the time is up, check your results. Instead of being tiny and shriveled, the raisins are now fat and bloated. Reach in and squeeze a couple. How did they get so heavy and squishy?

Action, Reaction, Results

You are observing an example of **osmosis**. Water naturally moves from areas of greater concentration to areas of lesser **concentration**. In this case, the water travels through a **membrane**, the raisin skin. When you first put the raisins in the jar, lots of water was outside of each dried-up raisin and not much inside. The water moved through tiny openings in the raisin skin deep into the raisin itself, making it heavy, soft, and bloated.

Something Extra

If you sit in a tub of water for a long time, your fingers probably will get wrinkly. Why doesn't your whole body undergo the same change? While you're in the tub, your skin will absorb some water, but much of your skin is partly protected from absorbing water by an oily substance called sebum. This substance is produced by tiny glands known as sebaceous glands. They occur all over the body, except in the skin of your fingertips and toes. As a result, water enters those areas by osmosis, and the skin there becomes wrinkly like a prune and puffy.

Try to figure out a way to prevent osmosis from taking place in this experiment. Hint: As sebum helps keep water from being absorbed through our skin, think of a substance that could do the same for the raisins. How about dipping the raisins in oil or painting them with clear nail polish before you begin? Try it and see!

A Hairy Sponge

This unusual garden grows so fast it will stand your hair on end. But can it really survive without soil?

Materials

- seeds (such as radish or alfalfa)
- small bowl
- water
- strainer
- kitchen sponge
- saucer
- spray bottle of water

Directions

❶ Place a handful of seeds in a small bowl and cover them with water. Let the seeds soak for about an hour, then pour them into a strainer to separate them from the water.

❷ Soak the sponge for a few moments in water, wring it out, and place it in the saucer.

❸ Sprinkle a handful of the wet seeds from the strainer on the sponge and poke them down into the openings.

❹ Place the saucer in a warm area, but not in direct sunlight. Using the spray bottle, keep the sponge moist over the next 2 or 3 days. The seeds will soon sprout, and tiny hairlike plants will shoot up. When your garden needs a trim, just munch away. It should stay fresh for a week or two.

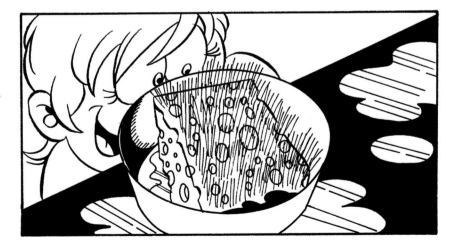

Action, Reaction, Results

Most plants make their own food with sunlight, air, and water in a process called **photosynthesis**. As they grow, they get other nutrients they need from the soil. When seed-bearing plants first begin to sprout, they are unable to use photosynthesis to produce food because their leaves are too immature to do so. Seeds, however, have a limited food supply inside them that helps get the new plants started. Once this food supply is used up, the seeds fall away from the new plants and decay. In this experiment the tiny plants in the sponge use the stored food in the seeds to get started. If you want to keep the plants going longer than a week or so, add a few drops of liquid fertilizer to the sponge or transplant them to your garden.

Something Extra

Seeds come in all sizes. The world's smallest seeds are those of certain orchids. They are so tiny that it takes more than 28 million of them to weigh an ounce. The heaviest seed is that of the coco-de-mer, found on the Seychelles Islands in the Indian Ocean. A single seed of this plant may weigh 44 pounds. Imagine trying to plant a row of those in your garden!

Bucket of Bacteria

The world would be a much stinkier place if we didn't bathe or brush our teeth. Here's a way to see why.

Materials

- ½ cup water
- saucepan
- small heat-proof bowl
- 4 packets unflavored gelatin
- mixing spoon
- glass jar with lid
- cotton swab

Directions

❶ Bring the water to a boil in saucepan, then, after it cools for a few minutes, pour carefully into the bowl.

❷ Sprinkle the 4 packets of gelatin into the bowl and stir until the powder dissolves.

❸ Pour the mixture into the jar, screw the lid on tightly, and set the jar on its side in a safe spot where it won't roll. Wait about 4 or 5 hours for the gelatin to set. (It is not necessary to put it in the refrigerator.)

❹ Now you need to find some bacteria. You won't have to look far! Take off your shoes and socks and rub the cotton swab between your toes. Now brush the swab across the gelatin in four long, separate strokes, then close the jar again and leave it in a warm, dark place for a few days.

❺ When you check your experiment, you won't see the bacteria, but you will see lines in the gelatin. The gelatin is what the bacteria have been eating. Now open the jar and stand back. The contents of the jar will smell terrible!

❻ When you are finished, dump the gelatin down the drain, followed by a rinse of hot water. Wash your hands and the inside of the jar thoroughly with soap and water.

❼ Repeat the steps again, but use a different source of bacteria. How about from your mouth or hands? Do you think you could collect bacteria from just-washed hands?

Action, Reaction, Results

There are billions of tiny organisms living on and around us called *bacteria*. Some are helpful, others are harmful, and still others are somewhere in between. For example, some bacteria on humans are responsible for unpleasant odors in the mouth, underarms, and feet.

The gelatin you prepared makes a good food source for such bacteria. It is called a *growth medium*. It allows the bacteria to reproduce easily, and you get the concentrated effect when you open the jar to smell it.

Something Extra

Bacteria are microscopic, single-celled **organisms***. Some are so tiny that it would take 50,000 of them to cover a square inch. They can also reproduce rapidly. Under ideal conditions, a single bacterium could possibly produce 3 billion new cells in a single day!*

Some very deadly diseases are caused by bacteria, including tetanus, leprosy, scarlet fever, and tuberculosis. On the other hand, life as we know it could not exist without certain bacteria, such as those that live in the human digestive system and help break down our food.

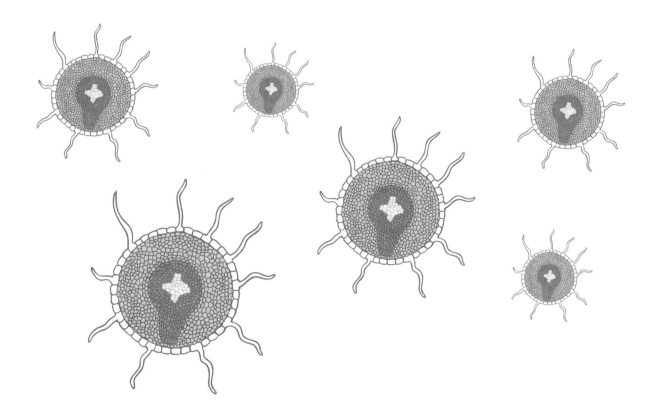

Which Way?

How does water get from the roots to the leaves?

Materials

- red food coloring
- glass jar
- pen
- 2 stalks of celery with leaves
- knife
- ruler

Directions

❶ Fill the jar with water and add a few drops of food coloring. Cut about an inch from the bottom of the celery and put the stalk in water.

❷ Check the stalk every half hour. What is happening? Can you see the food coloring traveling inside the stem? If you leave the celery in the jar for a while longer, will the coloring reach the leaves? Try it.

❸ Remove the stalk and cut another inch from the bottom. The small circles you see are the ends of fluid-filled tubes that run the length of the plant. These tubes are what carry the water to the leaves. The water in the tubes also keeps the plant stem firm.

❹ Pour out the colored water and wash the jar. Place the second stalk of celery in direct sunlight for a few hours. What happened to the water in the celery? Without water to support the stems how is the celery different?

❺ Fill the jar with fresh cool water and place the stalk in it. Leave it for an hour or so. Is the celery any different? Why?

Action, Reaction, Results

Tiny tubes, called XYLEM (zi-lem), in the stems and leaves of a green plant transport the water from the roots. Water is drawn up from the roots and carried to every part of the plant where it is needed. The water inside the xylem also helps to support the plant and keep it firm.

A Fungus Among Us

Here's an idea for a particularly disgusting gag lunch—a mold sandwich. No joke . . . the musty odor can really make you gag!

Materials

- slice of bread
- 1 teaspoon water
- small, flat plate
- self-sealing sandwich bag
- label
- pen
- notepad

Directions

❶ To dampen the slice of bread, pour the teaspoon of water on a flat plate and spread it around, getting as much of the plate wet as possible. Then lay the bread in it. If needed, sprinkle a little more water on the bread with a spoon.

❷ Remove the moist bread from the plate, slip it into the sandwich bag, and fasten the bag shut.

Wild & Wacky Science Experiments

❸ Put the bag in a warm, dark place for one week—a closet or cupboard will work. Label the bag with a warning such as *experiment in progress* to let your family know that it is an experiment and not lunch. Whatever you do, don't forget about it!

❹ Check once a day, every day, to see how the fungus is developing. If you wish, you can draw sketches or make notes about what you see so you have a record of the progress of the experiment. This will make it easier to see how quickly the fungus grows from day to day. At the end of the week you should find that the bread is covered with a layer of mold.

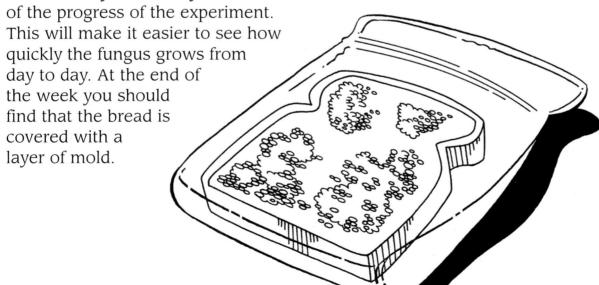

Action, Reaction, Results

Mold is a kind of **fungus**. It grows from spores (tiny cells with hard coverings) that are so small that they float on air. Even though you can't see them, spores are already on the bread before you put it in the bag. By putting water on the bread and placing it in a cupboard, you are creating the warm, damp environment that helps spores grow. Unlike green plants, fungi do not make their own food from sunlight, air, and water. Fungi live by absorbing food from other sources. *Fungus* is from a Latin term meaning "food-robbing."

Something Extra

Penicillin is an important life-saving medicine known as an **antibiotic***. Penicillin is produced by a mold. In 1928 a British scientist named Alexander Fleming noticed that a certain mold stopped the growth of bacteria. It took many years, but scientists finally isolated the important element that fought infection. Since then, penicillin—first discovered in a lowly mold—has helped save millions of lives.*

More Ways Than One

Do plants only grow from seeds?

Materials

- 2 jars
- knife
- white potato
- carrot (with some of the green top on it)
- water

Directions

❶ Cut the carrot about an inch from the top. Fill one of the jars with about $\frac{1}{2}$ inch of water. Place the carrot in the jar, cut side down. What part of the plant does the carrot come from? What do you think will happen?

❷ Cut the potato into sections. Be sure that each section has an "eye." Put two or three potato pieces into a glass jar with one-half inch of water in the bottom. What part of the plant does the potato come from?

❸ Put both jars in a sunny place. Add water when needed. After two or three days, what happens?

Action, Reaction, Results

You do not always have to plant seeds to grow a new plant. Some kinds of plants can grow from a section of the parent such as the leaves, stems, or roots. Other plants, such as mushrooms and ferns, grow from special cells called spores.

Jeepers, Check those Creeping Peepers

The small spud sits quietly in a corner. But what's happening? Are those long, spindly tentacles sprouting out of its eyes? It's the attack of the killer potato!

Materials

- potato, any kind with eyes
- knife
- clean jar or glass with opening wide enough to fit potato
- 4 toothpicks
- water

Directions

❶ Check your potato for firmness. It should be hard with no dark, soft, rotten spots. With an adult's help, slice off the lower third of the potato. (You can dispose of it or save it for a smaller version of this experiment.) Stick four toothpicks securely in the larger piece, spacing them evenly around the potato about ½ inch above the bottom flat end.

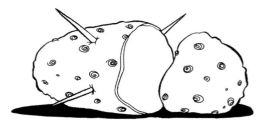

❷ Fill the jar nearly to the rim with cool tap water. Place the cut end of the potato in the water, with the toothpicks resting on the jar's opening.

❸ Put the jar in a warm place that gets sunlight for at least an hour or two each day. Check every other day to be sure the water continues to cover the cut end of the potato.

❹ In about a week the potato will sprout leaves and roots from little depressions known as *eyes*. If you want to keep your new plant, let it grow to about 6 inches tall, then plant about an inch of the root end of the potato in a pot of soil. Place it in a sunny location, keeping the soil moist, and your pet plant will flourish.

Action, Reaction, Results

Vegetative propagation, demonstrated in this experiment, is the term for growing a new plant from a part of an adult plant rather than from seeds or **spores**.

Although a potato grows underground, it is not a root or a seed. It is actually a tuber, or food storage unit, for the potato plant. A tuber is the enlarged end of an underground stem. When conditions are right, the eyes on the potato can sprout leaves and roots, growing into a new plant. At first, the plant is nourished by the "meat" of the potato (the part we eat), which is mostly water, starch, and some **protein**. Once the new young plant is well established with a system of leaves and roots, it is nourished by the soil that it is planted in.

Something Extra
If you wanted to grow potatoes in your garden, you probably would not plant seeds, because potato plants grown from seeds can vary tremendously. Instead you would plant small pieces of potato called sets. Each set must include at least one eye. The plants grown from pieces of potato are identical to the parent plant. It's almost like cloning in your own backyard!

Muggy, Muddy Waters

Create a murky swamp, then clean it up without even breaking a sweat. (Just wait until you see the muddy mess this experiment leaves behind!)

Materials

- 2 cereal bowls
- water
- 2 tablespoons of dirt
- mixing spoon
- brick (or shoe box)
- white handkerchief

Directions

❶ Fill one cereal bowl halfway with water, then add 2 tablespoons of dirt and stir well.

❷ Put the brick (or upside-down shoe box) on a flat surface and set the bowl of muddy water on top of it. Place the empty second bowl on the flat surface next to the brick, so it rests several inches below the muddy water.

❸ Roll the handkerchief into a tube, tight enough to stay rolled up. Place one end of the handkerchief in the muddy water and the other end in the empty bowl, not quite touching the bottom.

❹ Wait 24 hours, then check the experiment. How did the water get into the once-empty bowl? Where is the dirt?

Action, Reaction, Results

You are looking at an example of **capillary action**. Say what? It's like this: The cloth is made up of tiny fibers with air spaces in between. The water slowly creeps up into the spaces, a little higher on the sides than in the middle, giving the water level a cup shape. The water molecules attract each other, soon drawing the center of the water surface up the cloth, causing the entire waterline to become level. When that happens, the water on the sides creeps up again and so on, until the water makes it over the edge of the bowl. Gravity takes over and the water slowly seeps down the hanky, finally dripping into the lower bowl. The dirt is left behind because it's too heavy to hitch a ride up the hanky.

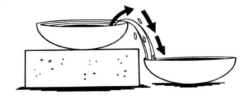

Important! *No matter how clean the water in the lower bowl looks, don't drink it. The dirt may have been too heavy to make the trip, but lightweight **bacteria** might have hitched a ride and could make you sick if you drink the water.*

Something Extra

Water rises in plant stems and tree trunks by capillary action. For some trees, the journey of the water to the top is a pretty impressive trip. For example, the tallest tree in the United States stands in Redwood National Park, Orick, California, and measures more than 365 feet tall.

Wiggle and Squirm

Amaze your friends by using capillary action to turn a plain paper wrapper into a wiggly worm.

Materials

- drinking straw with a paper wrapper
- cup of water

Directions

❶ Hold the wrapped straw upright on a tabletop. Tear the paper wrapper from the exposed tip.

❷ Slide the wrapper down so that it bunches up around the base of the straw. Slip the wrapper off and place the tightly squeezed paper on its side on the tabletop.

❸ Dip one end of the straw about $\frac{1}{2}$-inch deep into the cup of water. Capture a few drops of water in the straw by placing your index finger over the open end.

❹ Hold the straw over the scrunched wrapper and carefully drip water along its length.

Action, Reaction, Results

The paper seems to wriggle and squirm as if it were alive! The process at work here is capillary action. Paper and cloth are made up of tiny fibers that have small spaces in between them. These fibers absorb, or suck up, the water by a process called capillary action. Water molecules move through the spaces adhering to the fibers. As the water molecules move along the fibers, they attract other water molecules. As the crunched fibers in the paper wrapper soak up water, they straighten out and the paper lengthens.

Energy You Can See

What color is light?

Materials

- tall glass
- 3 x 5 inch index card (white)
- scissors
- tape
- large sheet of white paper

Directions

❶ A beam of white light is made up of many colors that our brain perceives as one. To break a beam of light into its individual colors, cut a one-inch-wide three-inch-long rectangle from a white 3 x 5 inch index card with the scissors.

❷ Tape the card to the glass so that the opening is directly over the rim.

❸ Fill the glass with water and set it on the ledge or on a table in front of a sunny window. Place the white paper on the floor in front of the glass. The colors will be reflected individually onto the white card under the glass. How many colors do you see? These colors make up the visible spectrum.

Action, Reaction, Results

Sunlight is made up of many different colors of light. Each of these different colors vibrate at a slightly different speed. When the sunlight passes through the water in the glass, each of the colors is slowed and bent. The colors that vibrate faster are bent more than the colors that vibrate slower. Blue and violet rays bend the most, and red the least.

Coin in a Cup

How can you move a coin without touching it? If you put a coin on a table, it will stay there until someone or something moves it. We say the coin has inertia. Every object in the universe has inertia. This means that an object that is not moving will stay that way until something moves it. An object that is moving will keep moving in the same direction until something stops it.

Materials

- small plastic cup
- flat surface
- 3 x 5 inch index card
- coin (nickel or quarter)

Directions

❶ Place the cup on a flat surface.

❷ Center the index card over the top of the cup.

❸ Place the coin in the middle of the card.

❹ Quickly flick your index finger against the edge of the card. What happens?

Action, Reaction, Results

At the beginning of the experiment, the cup, the card, and the coin were all motionless. Because of inertia, they remained where they were. When you flicked the card with your finger, the card flew off and the coin dropped into the cup. The flick of your finger was a force, or type of power, that moved the card. You did not touch the coin or cup, so they did not move. Once the card was gone, however, the force of gravity pulled the coin down.

Something Extra

Place a plastic cup on its side on a flat surface. Put a marble into the cup. Quickly push the cup forward about a foot, then stop it suddenly. The marble will roll out of the cup. Why does that happen?

Moaning Marvin

When Marvin gets going, the whine of his wooden head can send chills up and down your spine.

Materials

- rectangle of pine or other light wood, approximately 8 inches long, 2 inches wide, and $\frac{1}{4}$ inch thick
- 3-foot length of $\frac{1}{8}$-inch-thick string
- drill or hammer and large nail
- colored markers

Directions

❶ Ask an adult to help you make a hole in one end of the block of wood just large enough to pass the string through. Using a drill is the easiest way, but it also can be done with a hammer and a large nail.

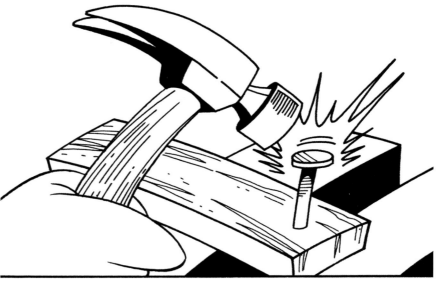

❷ Draw a scary face on the wood with the markers.

❸ Pass the string through the hole and tie the end securely with double knots. Have an adult check your work—you don't want to launch Marvin into orbit in the middle of the experiment!

❹ To perform the experiment you must move outside, at least 10 feet away from buildings, trees, and people. Grip the loose end of the string and whirl the wood in a large circle above your head. Check out the spooky moaning sound Marvin makes!

Action, Reaction, Results

There are a couple of things at work here. The moaning **sound** is created because the wood and cord vibrate as they move through the air, causing the surrounding air to vibrate. These air vibrations travel in waves and eventually strike a membrane in your ear called your *eardrum*. The vibrations are then passed on to nerve endings in your inner ear and you hear the vibrations as sound. Because Marvin is moving in a circle, the vibrations repeat at intervals that make a sound like a moan.

The force that keeps Marvin going in a circle instead of flying off into space is called **centripetal force**. Objects tend to want to keep moving in a straight line, unless a force makes them change direction. Your arm and the string are applying that force to Marvin.

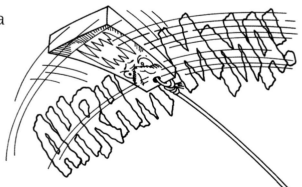

Something Extra

*If you slow down or speed up, you can change the **pitch** of the moan. Pitch is a measure of the **frequency** of vibrations. Try spinning Marvin at different speeds to see how the sound changes.*

Sneaky Snakes

What could be scarier than hearing the rattle of a rattlesnake? Holding the source of that disturbing sound in your hands!

Materials

- needle-nose pliers
- piece of strong wire about 5 inches long (coat-hanger wire works well)
- two 3-inch-long rubber bands
- metal washer, approximately 1 inch in diameter
- paper coin-envelope
- pencil
- an unsuspecting friend

Directions

❶ Using the pliers, curl the two ends of the wire as shown. Make a small bend in the center of the wire, forming an open-ended triangle.

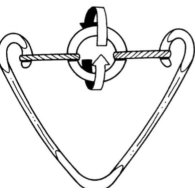

❷ Thread one rubber band halfway through the hole in the washer, then hook both ends of the band onto one curved end of the wire. Repeat the process on the other wire end with the second rubber band, threading it through the same washer.

❸ Take the coin envelope and write BEWARE: Snake! in large letters. Now turn the washer about twenty times as you would turn the winder on a windup toy. Slip the entire contraption into the coin envelope, being careful not to let the bands unwind. Keep the washer flat and slip the flap of the envelope inside.

❹ Hand your prepared envelope to a friend and say, "Open this envelope if you dare!" Your friend will have to reach in to pull out the flap. That will release the washer and it will spin, making a disturbing rattlesnake sound in the paper envelope.

Action, Reaction, Results

This experiment is a demonstration of potential and kinetic **energy**. Energy is the ability to do work. **Potential energy** is the possible energy something has because of its position. When the position changes, the object can accomplish work. For example, a ball at the top of a staircase has potential energy. Give it a nudge, and as the ball tumbles down the stairs, its potential energy changes to **kinetic energy**. Kinetic energy is the energy of motion, or energy that is at work. In Sneaky Snakes, the washer and the tightly wound rubber bands have potential energy until the washer is released, then the spinning washer and unwinding rubber bands have kinetic energy.

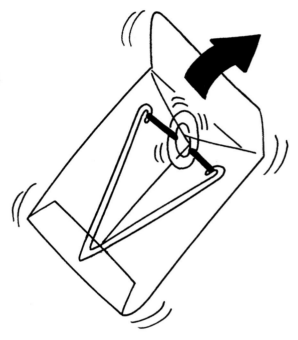

Something Extra

*Energy can be stored in two main ways. One is the potential energy a body has because of its position. Another way energy can be stored is as **chemical energy**, or the energy stored in an **atom** or molecule, which can be released through a **chemical reaction**. Examples of stored chemical energy are gas in a car or food in your body. When you run around, the chemical energy in the food you have eaten is released. About 25 percent of it is changed to kinetic energy. Most of it is converted to heat so the body has to find ways to cool itself down. Which brings us to a gross side-effect of using up all this energy—sweat. In fact, if you lived in a hot climate and played hard all day, you could sweat out as much as 12 quarts of fluid in a day.*

Charge It

Do electrically charged objects attract nonmetal objects?

Materials

- plastic comb
- small bits of paper
- wool fabric

Directions

❶ Hold the comb over the small pieces of paper for a moment. Does anything happen? Turn on the kitchen tap slowly so that there is a steady stream of water. Hold the comb as close to the stream as you can without getting it wet. Does anything happen now?

❷ Rub the comb briskly with the wool fabric.

❸ Hold it over the pieces of paper. They stick to the comb.

④ Rub the comb again with the wool and hold it near the stream of water. What happens this time? The comb contains a stored charge of static electricity. It attracts things with a different charge.

⑤ Lightning is caused by static electricity. To make your own lightning, turn on the kitchen tap after dark. Comb your hair several times, then place the comb near running water. A spark will jump from the comb to the water. You will see the spark more easily if you don't turn on the light. This experiment will work best when the weather is dry.

Action, Reaction, Results

One of the most basic properties of electricity is charge. Charge can be negative or positive. Objects with opposite charge are attracted to each other and those with like charge repel. Electrons have a negative charge. They are tiny particles that orbit the center of atoms. Protons (tiny particles in the center of atoms) have a positive charge. An atom with fewer electrons than protons is positively charged. An atom with more electrons than protons is negatively charged. Atoms with an even number of both are neutral. Static electricity is the buildup of either negative or positive charge in a substance.

Like Magic

Can static electricity do work?

Materials

- 5 x 5 inch square of paper
- thread
- 1 sharp pencil
- comb
- piece of wool fabric
- 2 balloons
- modeling clay
- scissors

Directions

❶ Fold the paper and cut it as shown in the drawing to form a star. Push the eraser end of the pencil into the ball of clay so that it will stand. Balance the paper star on the point of the pencil.

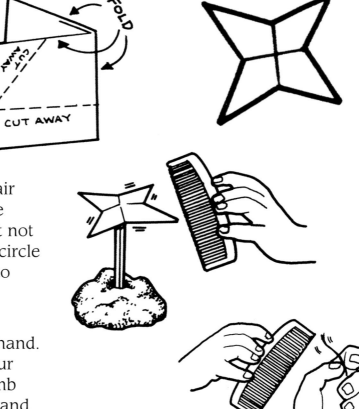

❷ Run the comb through your hair several times or rub it with the fabric. Hold the comb near but not touching the star and make a circle around it. The star will begin to move. Do you know what is causing it to spin?

❸ Hold a piece of thread in one hand. With the other hand, comb your hair quickly, then pass the comb over the thread. It will rise up and follow the comb. The thread is attracted to the comb.

❹ Blow up both balloons and tie one to each end of a long piece of thread. Holding the thread in the center, allow the balloons to dangle. Do they touch? Quickly rub each balloon on your hair. Dangle the balloons again. Will they touch each other now?

Action, Reaction, Results

Protons always stay in the same place, but electrons can be made to move from one atom to another. Between certain materials, electrons move very easily. By running the comb through your hair or rubbing the balloons together, you are causing electrons to move from one place to another. The objects build up either a positive or negative charge depending on the materials you use.

Glossary

acid: A chemical compound containing hydrogen.

air pressure: The force exerted by the air in the atmosphere. It is approximately 15 pounds per square inch at sea level at 32°F.

aldehydes: A class of highly reactive organic chemicals.

antibiotic: A drug used to treat infections caused by bacteria or fungi.

antioxidants: Substances that prevent or delay chemical interaction with oxygen. Vitamin C is a natural antioxidant.

atom: The smallest unit of matter that cannot be divided by a chemical reaction.

bacteria: Single-celled, microscopic organisms. One of these organisms is called a bacterium.

base: A substance that reacts with an acid to form a salt.

capillary action: The rise or fall of liquids in narrow tubes.

centripetal force: A force that acts on a moving body that causes that body to move in a curved path.

chemical energy: Energy released by a chemical reaction.

chemical reaction: The interaction of two or more substances, which results in chemical changes in the substances.

compost: Decayed plant material that provides nutrients in the soil for growing plants.

concentration: The amount per unit volume of one substance in a given space or other substance.

contracts: Becomes smaller.

denatured: What happens when a protein is changed, chemically or by heat, causing the protein to lose its solubility.

density: The mass (amount of matter) of a substance (per unit volume).

embryo: Inside a plant seed, the first stage of a new plant, before it has begun to grow.

energy: The ability to do work.

enzyme: A protein in the body that helps a chemical reaction take place.

evaporates: Changes from a liquid to a gas through heat or air movement.

fluids: Substances that flow, such as liquid or gas. Fluids take the shape of the container holding them.

frequency: In sound waves, the number of waves per second.

friction: The resistance to motion between two surfaces.

fungus: A plantlike organism that has no chlorophyll and cannot produce its own food. Mushrooms, mold, and yeast are examples of fungi.

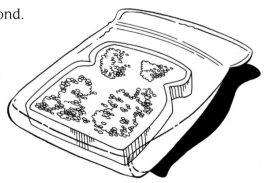

heat: A form of energy transferred from one body or substance to another of lower temperature. Heat is released by physical and chemical processes.

immiscible liquids: Liquids that do not mix together, such as oil and water.

kinetic energy: Energy possessed by a body by virtue of its motion.

lubricant: A substance used to reduce friction between moving parts. Oil is a lubricant.

matter: The substance of which all objects are made. Matter occupies space, has weight, and can exist as a solid, liquid, or gas.

membrane: A thin layer of tissue that surrounds, separates, and protects living cells. Plant and animal organs may be separated or lined by a membrane.

metamorphosis: A change from one state to another in the life cycle of certain organisms.

microorganisms: Living things too small to be seen without a microscope.

molecule: The smallest unit of a compound that can exist by itself and still have the properties of that compound.

organisms: Living things.

osmosis: The passage of a solvent from a less concentrated into a more concentrated solution through a membrane that only partly permits the liquids to pass through it.

photosynthesis: The process by which green plants produce food from air, water, and sunlight.

pitch: The highness or lowness of a sound. The greater the frequency of the sound waves, the higher the pitch.

potential energy: The energy a body or object possesses by virtue of its position.

protein: An organic compound containing amino acids. Proteins are necessary for the body to function.

scientific method: The way scientists learn and study the world around them. The scientific method is comprised of these steps: identify the problem; gather data; form a hypothesis; perform an experiment; analyze the data; draw a conclusion.

soluble: Able to be dissolved in a liquid.

solution: A liquid, gas, or solid in which one or more substances are dissolved.

sound: A vibration that travels through a gas, liquid, or solid, but not through empty space. The human ear detects the vibrations, and the human brain interprets the vibrations as sound.

spore: The reproductive cell of certain organisms such as fungi and some plants.

suspension: Particles of matter spread throughout but not dissolved in a liquid.

toxic: Poisonous.

vegetative propagation: The use of part of a plant, other than a seed, to produce a new plant.

viscosity: The resistance to movement within a fluid.

volume: The amount of space taken up by a substance or object.